Surprised

5

Simon Cansdale

with illustrations by
Taffy

Series Editor: James Jones

the bible reading fellowship
OPENING THE BIBLE

Surprise, surprise!

Rumpus the cat was a creature of habit.
Every morning he would sit on the first
floor landing of his house. At the end of
the landing there was a bathroom. In a
dazzling blur of fluff, Rumpus would
bound across the landing, through the
bathroom, on to the toilet seat, and
finally on to the window ledge. From
there he could watch the birds in
the garden. But one morning
Rumpus had a big surprise. A
visitor forgot to put down the
toilet seat. Rumpus didn't realize
until too late. Splash . . .!

What's the biggest surprise
you've had recently?

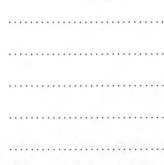

....

....

....

....

....

NOW WASH
YOUR PAWS

Elizabeth and Zechariah were happily married. They were getting old, but had no children, or grandchildren. One day, when he was working in the temple, Zechariah had the surprise of his life:

see that Zechariah couldn't believe the angel's news—he was too worried about how old he was! But because they trusted God together he used them to prepare the world for Jesus.

An angel of the Lord appeared to him, standing on the right of the altar where the incense was burnt. When Zechariah saw him, he was alarmed and felt afraid. But the angel said to him, 'Don't be afraid, Zechariah! God has heard your prayer, and your wife Elizabeth will bear you a son. You are to name him John. How glad and happy you will be, and how happy many others will be when he is born! He will be a great man in the Lord's sight.'

Luke 1:11–15

Lord, when you took Elizabeth and Zechariah by surprise they kept on trusting you. Help me to keep on trusting you even when things don't turn out the way I expect. Amen.

This news took Elizabeth and Zechariah by surprise—even though they had prayed for a son.

They were an unlikely couple for God to choose. Elizabeth looked too old to have a baby. Yet God decided that they should bring up the person who would introduce his Son, Jesus, to the world.

This shows that you can never predict how God is going to work or who he'll choose.

Nor do you have to get it right first time. If you read on in Luke 1 you can

'No one tells me what to do!' That was Alison's favourite phrase. She did her own thing. If she served anyone, she served herself. Many of her friends looked up to her, impressed at her independence.

Compare her to Mary, Jesus' mother. Few people were more surprised by Jesus than her. When the angel Gabriel told her that she would have a baby, she was amazed. She wasn't even married then, and hadn't slept with her future husband Joseph. So how could she have a baby?

Gabriel also said that her child would be unique—she would give birth to God's Son, not Joseph's. How would Alison have reacted to this news?

- ☐ What will my parents say?
- ☐ Joseph won't believe me.
- ☐ I'm too young to be pregnant.
- ☐ I'm not going to ruin my life.
- ☐ I am ready to serve God in this way.

Ready to serve

List one thing about living as a Christian that you find hard. Something that makes you unpopular or that takes up your time.

. . . .

. . . .

Think quietly about what you have written. Why do you find it difficult?

. . . .

. . . .

Repeat Mary's words—'I am the Lord's servant.'

Pray that God would set you free as you serve him.

This is what Mary said:

'I am the Lord's servant,' said Mary; 'may it happen to me as you have said.'

Luke 1:38

Mary showed how we should respond to God—quietly and happily. She risked serving God instead of herself. She discovered, unlike Alison, that this is the best way to be free.

Oh God, the author of peace and lover of friendship, to know you is eternal life, to serve you is perfect freedom. Amen.

Shepherds have a hard life. They work outside in all conditions. They must find water and grass for their flock. They sometimes chase off wild animals, and pull their sheep and goats out of ditches and hedges.

This was as true in Jesus' day as it is now. What's more, people made rude jokes about shepherds, and treated them as outcasts because they often stole their master's sheep.

But it was to shepherds that God decided to break the news about the birth of his son Jesus. Shepherds—before all the big important people of the day.

 Read Luke 2:10–12

Don't be afraid! I am here with good news for you, which will bring great joy to all the people. This very day in David's town your Saviour was born—Christ the Lord! And this is what will prove it to you: you will find a baby wrapped in strips of cloth and lying in a manger.

The Saviour had been born! They would find him wrapped in rags in a feeding trough. No palace, no fine clothes, no royal doctors. Not even a hot bath or a proper bed! God's chosen one (that's what 'Christ' means) had been born in a barn. God's Son came to earth as a helpless child, born to poor parents in the same room as farm animals.

If Jesus was born today, who do you think God would tell first?

....

What kind of people would his parents be, and where would he be born?

....

....

If you belong to a youth group why not suggest that you put on a nativity play at Christmas this year? Make it a modern version, as if it were taking place now where you live.

Here is a list of the main characters. In the right hand column put the initials of those you'd choose to take the part.

Herod ....

Shepherd 1 ....

Shepherd 2 ....

Shepherd 3 ....

Wise man 1 ....

Wise man 2 ....

Wise man 3 ....

Mary ....

Joseph ....

Born in a barn

Lord Jesus Christ, thank you for giving up everything to become like me. Help me to give up my life for others. Amen.

4

Anyone seen Jesus?

'You don't understand...!' Use the lines below to write about a time when you were misunderstood. How did you feel?

....

....

....

....

....

....

 Jesus was misunderstood by his parents when he was a young boy. The story reveals two surprises about Jesus:

Every year the parents of Jesus went to Jerusalem for the Passover Festival. When Jesus was twelve years old, they went to the festival as usual. When the festival was over, they started back home, but the boy Jesus stayed in Jerusalem. His parents did not know this; they thought that he was with the group, so they travelled a whole day and then started looking for him among their relatives and friends. They did not find him so they went back to Jerusalem looking for him. On the third day they found him in the Temple, sitting with the Jewish teachers, listening to them and asking questions. All who heard him were amazed at his intelligent answers. His parents were astonished when they saw him, and his mother said to him, 'My son, why have you done this to us? Your father and I have been terribly worried trying to find you.' He answered them, 'Why did you have to look for me? Didn't you know that I had to be in my Father's house?'

Luke 2:41–49

Firstly, the Jewish teachers were amazed at Jesus' sharp questions and understanding of the Old Testament. Jesus was starting to show his great wisdom and desire to express the truth about the world.

Secondly, his parents were surprised. He said that they should have known that he would be in his *'Father's house '*. But wasn't his father Joseph standing right next to him? Jesus knew that God was his true Father. It was right that he spent special time with him.

Mary and Joseph did not then understand what Jesus meant. Jesus was underlining his personal relationship with God, his Father. Later in his life, this was what most struck many people who met him.

But it is not a closed relationship. Jesus invites all of us to enjoy the same closeness with God. We can call God *'Father'* too.

Loving Father, thank you that we can join in Jesus' relationship with you. Thank you that we can call you 'Father'. Amen.

5

Which of these words is the odd one out?

Trust
Loyalty
Damage
Close
Sharing
Friendship

After Jesus was baptized, the devil tried to damage Jesus' relationship with God. He knew that if he could stop Jesus loving and obeying his Father, he would ruin all that Jesus had come to do.

Read Luke 4:5–8

Then the Devil took him up and showed him in a second all the kingdoms of the world. 'I will give you all this power and all this wealth,' the Devil told him. 'It has all been handed over to me, and I can give it to anyone I choose. All this will be yours, then, if you worship me.' Jesus answered, 'The scripture says, "Worship the Lord your God and serve only Him!"'

The devil lied—the world was not his to give. He lied and offered Jesus the chance of great power, if only he would turn his back on his Father.

Jesus knew immediately what the devil was up to. He said clearly that he would stay obedient to God. He would not betray the trust and openness they enjoyed. He would not give in to lies and shallow hopes of power.

Not many of us are tempted to take over as rulers of the world. But we're tempted to damage our relationship with God. Or misuse what he has given to us.

Under

Jesus valued obeying God and being true to his commands more than evil, empty promises.

Which one of these areas are you most tempted in?

☐ gossip
☐ being selfish
☐ pretending not to be a Christian
☐ hurting other people
☐ swearing
☐ telling lies
☐ other . . . .

How does this damage your relationship with God?

. . . .

. . . .

Rearrange the letters to discover what you can do to face this temptation:

SAK . . . . yourself what God wants you to do by DERAING . . . . the Bible or LKIGNTA . . . . with a Christian friend.
Be DENIETOB . . . . to what God wants.
YARP . . . . for God's strength to help you.

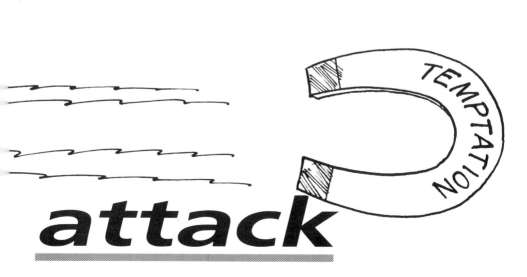

Lord Jesus, you know how hard it is to face temptation. Please show me how to follow you. Please give me strength to resist temptation and be obedient to you. Amen.

attack

6

Imagine you want to be elected to your school Parliament. Write a one-sentence slogan for yourself. Something to explain what you stand for:

. . . .

. . . .

. . . .

 Jesus had a 'manifesto' too. He chose some verses from the Old Testament:

The Spirit of the Lord is upon me, because he has chosen me to bring good news to the poor.
He has sent me to proclaim liberty to the captives,
and recovery of sight for the blind;
to set free the oppressed
and announce that the time has come when the Lord will save his people.

Luke 4:18–19

Jesus first read these words to people from his own village, Nazareth. They were impressed. What great ideas! But they couldn't believe that Jesus was going to carry them out. '*After all,*' they said, '*it's only Jesus, Joseph's son—we've known him since he was a lad. What's so special about him?*'

But look carefully at Jesus' words. They weren't empty promises or just fine ideas to impress people.
Jesus was filled with the Holy Spirit when John baptized him (Luke 3). For the next three years he shared God's good news with people like Zacchaeus (Luke 19) and a paralysed man (Luke 5). He set free a man tormented by evil sprits (Luke 8), and gave sight to a blind beggar (Luke 18). He gave freedom and forgiveness to a sinful woman (Luke 7).

VOTE JESUS!

By what he said, and what he did, he put God's rescue plan for the world into action.

If you belong to a Youth Group, why not make your own manifesto?

☐ Look together at Jesus' manifesto. What did he set out to do?
☐ How can you, his followers, do the same in your community?
☐ Put your ideas into a short, clear manifesto.
☐ Ask to see the leaders of your church and talk about what you can do together.

Lord Jesus, please show me what I can do to love other people the way that you did. Amen.

HMMM?

7

Come on board!

Read Luke 5:4–10

When he finished speaking, he said to Simon, 'Push the boat out further to the deep water, and you and your partners let down your nets for a catch.' 'Master,' Simon answered, 'we worked hard all night long and caught nothing. But if you say so, I will let down the nets.' They let them down and caught such a large number of fish that the nets were about to break. So they motioned to their partners in the other boat to come and help them. They came and filled both boats so full of fish that the boats were about to sink. When Simon Peter saw what had happened, he fell on his knees before Jesus and said, 'Go away from me, Lord! I am a sinful man!' . . . Jesus said to Simon, 'Don't be afraid; from now on you will be catching men.'

Andy didn't like the word 'sin'. It made him feel uncomfortable and angry. He wasn't a sinner. Only murderers were sinners!

But something made Andy change his mind. Some friends dragged him along to hear a talk about Jesus. He expected to be bored. But he was gripped. His own life didn't seem so perfect now. He cried at the way he had insulted and ignored God. How could God accept him?

Simon Peter, one of Jesus' followers, felt like this several times. Simon was a fisherman. Always had been, always will be—so he thought. But one day Jesus arrived. That soon changed things. Jesus needed somewhere to sit to talk to the crowds, so he borrowed Simon's boat.

Simon Peter was a hard guy. He didn't often get down on his knees in public. But when he heard Jesus preach, and saw the unbelievable catch of fish, he was stunned. What amazing power and authority! He felt too dirty to be in Jesus' company.

Jesus agreed with Simon—yes, he was sinful. But instead of leaving, as Simon asked, he stayed. He invited Simon to be part of his new team. He would still be fishing, but this time for God, not his supper!

The same is true for Andy. He knows that he is far from perfect. He also knows that God loves him, and has a part for him to play in his kingdom.

So don't wait until you're perfect before you start fishing for God! You'll be waiting forever. Start now!

Most church services have a time of 'confession'—when we say sorry to God for things we have or have not done. Write a prayer of confession for your church. Ask if it can be used in one of the services.

Here's an example from the Old Testament:

*Be merciful to me, O God,
because of your constant love . . .
Remove my sin, and I will be clean;
wash me, and I will be whiter than
snow . . .
Create a pure heart in me, O God,
and put a new and loyal spirit in me.*

Psalm 51:1, 7, 10

You can't do that!

'I'm sorry, all the tickets are sold. You're too late.' Unbelievable! You've queued half the night to see your favourite band play at Wembley Arena, and now you can't get in! But just as you turn to go, someone wearing a leather jacket and dark glasses comes up to you, smiles, and gives you a ticket for the front row. *'Oh, and come back stage afterwards and meet the rest of the band. Just say I invited you. '*

What would you do?
- [ ] ignore them—they probably stole the ticket anyway
- [ ] ask how much
- [ ] tell them you can only get tickets from the box-office
- [ ] take it and go inside

 Read Luke 5:18–21

Some men came carrying a sick man on a bed . . . because of the crowd, however, they could find now way to take him in. So they carried him up on the roof, made an opening in the tiles, and let him down on his bed in the middle of the group in front of Jesus. When Jesus saw how much faith they had, he said to the man, 'Your sins are forgiven, my friend.' The Teachers of the Law and the Pharisees began to say to themselves, 'Who is this man who speaks such blasphemy? God is the only one who can forgive sins!'

HOI !! WHO'S GOING TO FIX MY ROOF ?

The religious leaders were amazed that Jesus dared to forgive the man's sins. He wasn't allowed to—only God could do that! But just as the lead-singer of a band can invite you back-stage at Wembley, because of who they are, so Jesus can forgive the sick man, because he was God's Son.

 *Read Luke 5:22–25*

> *Jesus knew their thoughts and said to them, 'Why do you think such things? Is it easier to say, "Your sins are forgiven you," or to say, "Get up and walk"? I will prove to you, then, that the Son of Man has authority on earth to forgive sins.' So he said to the paralysed man, 'I tell you, get up, pick up your bed and go home!' At once the man got up in front of them all, took the bed he had been lying on, and went home, praising God.*

Jesus challenged the doubters by healing the man right in front of them. But it was his power to forgive the man that took their breath away.

Jesus had the authority and power to heal not just the man's body, but his soul as well. He showed that whether our bodies are perfect or falling apart, we all need God's healing and forgiveness. Jesus heals the part of us that does the thinking, hoping, hating and lying—our inner self that we hide away because our friends and family would be shocked if they saw it.

Lord Jesus, I know that I can trust you to forgive me. Thank you that I can be sure of you. Amen.

9

Jenny had some homework to do for school the next day. And her room was in a mess. So she hoovered her room. Then she tidied up her school books. She sharpened all her pencils. She cleaned the basin. She even dusted the shelves. But it was no good. By the time she'd finished tidying up, it was time to go to bed. She didn't even start the homework!

What do you think her teacher would have said when she got to school?

. . . .

. . . .

 Read Luke 10:38–42

As Jesus and his disciples went on their way, he came to a village where a woman named Martha welcomed him in her home. She had a sister named Mary, who sat down at the feet of the Lord and listened to his teaching. Martha was upset over all the work she had to do, so she came and said, 'Lord, don't you care that my sister has left me to do all the work by myself. Tell her to come and help me!' The Lord answered her, 'Martha, Martha! You are worried and troubled over so many things, but just one is needed. Mary has chosen the right thing, and it will not be taken away from her.'

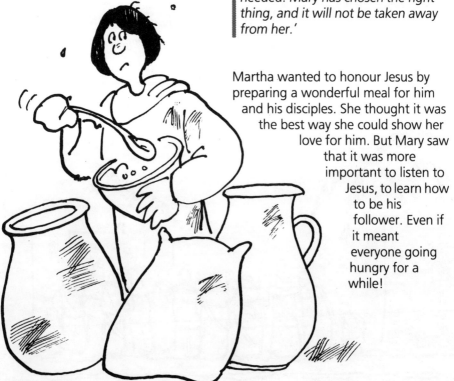

Martha wanted to honour Jesus by preparing a wonderful meal for him and his disciples. She thought it was the best way she could show her love for him. But Mary saw that it was more important to listen to Jesus, to learn how to be his follower. Even if it meant everyone going hungry for a while!

Being a good hostess and looking after people is a good thing. But it was getting in the way of Martha and enjoying Jesus' company and learning from him.

Tick the things on this list that distract you from following Jesus, or add your own:

Lord Jesus, sometimes my life is so full of things that are important to me that I push you to one side. Thank you for showing Martha that being with you comes first. Amen.

- ☑ Television
- ☑ Sport
- ☐ Friends
- ☐ Schoolwork
- ☐ Music/pop-stars
- ☐ Your image
- ☐ Other . . . .

. . . .

. . . .

Not now, I'm busy!

10 Out to dinner

Jesus was invited out to meals a lot. He was the sort of person everyone wanted to meet. Once he went to dinner with a man called Simon.

Simon thought of himself as rather important. So he didn't bother to welcome Jesus properly, or give him water to clean his feet (that was the polite thing to do in those days). But when they sat down to eat, something rather embarrassing happened.

A local woman knelt beside Jesus. She was crying, and wet his feet with her tears. Then she dried his feet with her hair, kissed them, and poured perfume on them.

Tick the word(s) that you think best describe how Simon and Jesus felt (or add your own):

 Read Luke 7:41–43

	Simon	Jesus
Embarrassed	✓	
Flattered . . .		
Glad		✓
Confused . .	✓	
Other:		happy

'There were two men who owed money to a money-lender,' Jesus began. 'One owed him five hundred silver coins, and the other owed him fifty. Neither of them could pay him back, so he cancelled the debts of both. Which one, then, will love him more?' 'I suppose,' said Simon, 'that it would be the one who was forgiven more.'

Rearrange the letters and circle who you think Jesus was talking about in this short story?

Both Simon and the woman needed the forgiveness of Jesus. The woman's love for Jesus showed that she knew he had forgiven her. Simon was so proud, he didn't even realize he had a problem.

Christians are not 'good' people. They are bad people who love God because he has forgiven them.

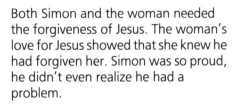

HTE MAWON

THE WOMAN

Lord Jesus, you have forgiven me and made me clean. I give my life back to you. Thank you for loving me. Amen.

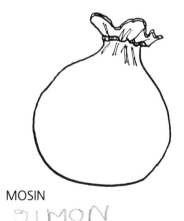

MOSIN

SIMON

A RICH

Write down one thing that you think it is impossible to do:

walk upside
down on the ceiling

A rich man once approached Jesus and asked him how he could get into heaven. But he was terribly disappointed. Jesus said that he should sell all he had, give the money away, and follow him with the other disciples. The man didn't want to give up that much.

Jesus saw that he was sad and said, 'How hard it is for rich people to enter the Kingdom of God! It is much harder for a rich person to enter the Kingdom of God than for a camel to go through the eye of a needle.' The people who heard him asked, 'Who, then, can be saved?' Jesus answered, 'What is impossible for man is possible for God.'

Luke 18:24–25

Why do you think Jesus said it is so hard for rich people to be saved?

☑ They are too selfish
☐ No one, rich or poor, can be saved by what they do
☐ They are too fat
☑ They think that they can buy their way into heaven

It is impossible for anyone to be saved by their own hard work or ready cash. No matter how much they give away to charity. Jesus used the example of the rich man to show this. He had led a fairly 'good' life. Couldn't he use his money to do more great things? To earn himself a place in heaven? No. If he couldn't be saved by what he did, then no one could. It was about as likely as fitting a camel

SEWING
NEEDLES
MADE
HERE

MAN

we can cheerfully accept Jesus' invitation to 'come and follow me', and his gift of new life.

through the eye of a needle— impossible! But Jesus loved this rich man. He wanted to show him that he couldn't buy his way into God's kingdom.

The disciples had learnt what the rich man didn't want to know. We can do nothing to save ourselves. Money, talent, good looks, the best education, popularity—none of these makes a difference to God. Like the disciples,

Lord Jesus, I'm sorry for the times when I've pretended that I'm good enough to get into heaven all on my own. I want to follow you like the disciples did. Please help me to do this. Amen.

Nobody likes to be ignored, or to feel an outsider. Zacchaeus, a chief tax collector from Jericho, was no different. He had few friends, because he cheated people and worked for the hated Romans.

Read Luke 19:1–6

> Jesus went on into Jericho and was passing through. There was a chief tax collector there named Zacchaeus, who was rich. He was trying to see who Jesus was, but he was a little man and could not see Jesus because of the crowd. So he ran ahead of the crowd and climbed a sycomore tree to see Jesus, who was going to pass that way. When Jesus came to that place, he looked up and said to Zacchaeus, 'Hurry down Zacchaeus, because I must stay in your house today.' Zacchaeus hurried down and welcomed him with great joy.

It's a big day in Jericho. Jesus is coming to town! People fill the streets, shouting and waving, trying to get close to him. A bit like when a famous pop-star arrives.

Imagine you work for Jericho Town Council. You're in charge of showing Jesus round for the day. Here is a list of people and places. Number the list from 1 to 6 to show which you would most like Jesus to see:

_2_ Lord Mayor
_4_ The local primary school
_3_ The hospital
_1_ Bouncing Bartimaeus and the Beeswax Boys, Jericho's no. 1 pop group
_6_ Zacchaeus, chief tax-collector
_5_ Jericho's new housing estate

There may have been many good and interesting people in Jericho that day. But Jesus chose one, only one, to stay with. Zacchaeus, the outsider, the one everybody hated. Jesus showed in his life that he cared deeply for people like Zacchaeus. Write down the initials of three people in your school/area who are unpopular:

C.V.   J.M.   R.L.

How can you surprise them, and show them the love of Jesus?

Holy Father, thank you for your love for all people. You know that I don't love those around me the same way that you do. Please fill me with your love. Amen.

Jesus comes to town

13

Brian the sheep has got lost in this maze of gates. Draw in the route that Peter the shepherd should take to find Brian.

How did this meeting with Jesus change Zacchaeus? Rearrange the letters to find out.

Used to be		Now
Selfish▷	erognesu	generous
A cheat▷	tehnos	honest
Lost▷	esvad	saved

Read Luke 19:7–10

All the people who saw it started grumbling, 'This man has gone as a guest to the home of a sinner!' Zacchaeus stood up and said to the Lord, 'Listen, sir! I will give half my belongings to the poor, and if I have cheated anyone, I will pay him back four times as much.' Jesus said to him, 'Salvation has come to this house today, for this man, also, is a descendant of Abraham. The Son of Man came to seek and to save the lost.'

Jesus told Zacchaeus that he had come to save people. Just like a shepherd that goes looking for sheep in wild country. Without Jesus the Shepherd we would all be lost and cut off from God.

On the following scales mark with the letter 'B' where you were before you became a Christian and 'A' where you are now:

Selfish							Generous		
1	2	3	4	5	6	7	(8)	9	10

A cheat								Honest	
1	2	3	4	5	6	7	8	(9)	10

Lost									Saved
1	2	3	4	5	6	7	8	9	(10)

Unhelpful									Kind
1	2	3	4	5	6	(7)	8	9	10

Lord Jesus, thank you for being like a shepherd, coming to look for lost sheep. Thank you for saving me. Amen.

An enthusiastic response

14

Read Luke 18:35–43

As Jesus was coming near Jericho, there was a blind man sitting by the road, begging. When he heard the crowd passing by, he asked, 'What is this?' 'Jesus of Nazareth is passing by,' they told him. He cried out, 'Jesus, Son of David! Take pity on me!' The people in front scolded him and told him to be quiet. But he shouted even more loudly, 'Son of David! Take pity on me!' So Jesus stopped and ordered the blind man to be brought to him.

When he came near, Jesus asked him, 'What do you want me to do for you?' 'Sir,' he answered, 'I want to see again.' Jesus said to him, 'Then see! Your faith has made you well.' At once he was able to see, and he followed Jesus, giving thanks to God. When the crowd saw it, they all praised God.

The crowd waiting for Jesus tried to keep this blind beggar quiet. Couldn't he see that he was being a real nuisance? Didn't he realize that Jesus had better things to do than to chat to some beggar?

But their efforts didn't work. Whether the beggar had heard Jesus speak before, or found out about the many people whom Jesus had healed, he definitely wanted to meet the man himself. No matter who shouted at him, or told him that Jesus wouldn't be interested.

He was right, of course. Imagine how the crowd felt when Jesus asked to meet him. Surely Jesus had got it wrong! Why should he want to talk to a blind beggar?

Jesus didn't only talk to the man. He gave him back his eyesight. This showed his power and authority—to heal a blind person at a touch. It also showed his care and concern for the poor and needy. Here was the Saviour, the Son of David, showing the love and power of God.

The blind man was determined to meet Jesus. Nothing would stop him. He found that Jesus was just as keen to meet him.

There's no one who's too small for Jesus to be bothered with. You don't have to have reached a certain standard before he's interested. Neither do you have to shout and scream to get his attention.

We can be sure that Jesus will hear us, and show us his love and power. For the blind man this meant a new life following Jesus and praising God, as well as being able to see again. Fill the blanks in this prayer to show how you would like Jesus to help you.

Lord Jesus, thank you that you care so deeply about people like the blind man in this story. Thank you for showing me the same love. You know that I need your help to . . . .

. . . . .

I want to keep on following you. Amen.

Shut up!

The disciples of Jesus found themselves in an impossible situation.

 Jesus had been speaking to a large crowd for most of the day:

When the sun was beginning to set, the twelve disciples came to him and said, 'Send the people away so that they can go to the villages and farms round here and find food and lodging, because this is a lonely place.' But Jesus said to them, 'You yourselves give them something to eat.' They answered, 'All we have are five loaves and two fish. Do you want us to go and buy food for this whole crowd?' (There were about five thousand men there.) Jesus said to the disciples, 'Make the people sit down in groups of about fifty each.' After the disciples had done so, Jesus took the five loaves and two fish, looked up to heaven, thanked God for them, and gave them to the disciples to distribute to the people. They all ate and had enough, and the disciples took up twelve baskets of what was left over.

Luke 9:12–17

The disciples learnt a crucial lesson. It didn't matter that they only had five loaves and two fish. What mattered was that they were working with Jesus. He used the little bit they had, and their willingness to work with him, to do a miracle.

It's easy to feel helpless when we think about serving God. It's easy to concentrate on how little we have to offer. But Jesus can make great use of this tiny amount. Working with him changes things completely.

One person who found this out was Elizabeth. She'd been so depressed that she wanted to die. But her life started to change when she decided to follow Jesus. *'God doesn't want me,'* she had thought. She was wrong. God showed her that she could share his love with other people. Very practically. Now she uses spare time after school and in the holidays to help out at a home for young children with mental disabilities. Everyone appreciates her love and kindness.

Write here, in the loaves and fishes, seven things you can offer God (like

Working with Jesus

spare time, money, enjoying music, painting or dancing, being a good friend or concerned for people who are left out):

Spend a few moments in silence. Picture the five loaves and two fish that the disciples gave to Jesus. Spend time offering each of your seven things to God. Ask God to use them for his work.

Spend a few moments in silence. Picture the twelve baskets of food left over after the meal. Thank God that he can use your small offering in the same way.

16

Name a film you've seen recently in which the hero gets revenge against people who've hurt him/her or others close to them.

Beethoven

Now name a film in which the hero shows love and concern for people who've hurt him/her.

Christy

(there aren't many!)

Jesus knew that when we're upset or angry we want to get back at the people who've hurt us. Many people would say that this is the 'natural' and best way to respond. It's certainly the way that most of our film heroes behave.

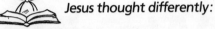

Jesus thought differently:

> *But I tell you who hear me: Love your enemies, do good to those who hate you, bless those who curse you, and pray for those who ill-treat you.*
>
> Luke 6:27–28

Yes, that's right; Jesus said that we should love our enemies and help them out! This is far more than saying:

▷ I won't beat up people I don't like
▷ I won't lie about others
▷ I won't try to make them suffer.

It's actively loving them in the same way as you love your friends. That is, looking out for what's good for them, and praying for them.

This is the way Jesus himself loved people. It meant that he would trust close friends even when they deserted him, and forgive the Roman soldiers who killed him.

KILLER REVENGE CERT 18

Write in the box the initials of someone you don't like:

> C V

Ask the following questions:

What can I do for this person this week?

Tell them their
good at something

What can I pray for them?

That the don
will fint to like him

Lord Jesus, you know that I find it very difficult to love . . . . Please help me to love them the same way you love me. Amen.

Now spend a minute praying for this person on your own. Use the ideas that you've written down for the second question.

Love
who?

17

Which three of the following do you most often find something wrong with?

☑ School .*too much work*

☑ Friends.... *bit stupid*

☐ Yourself...........................

☐ Magazines ....

☑ Television .*bad language*

☐ Famous people ....

Write next to each what it is that you don't like.

Jesus said:

Why do you look at the speck in your brother's eye, but pay no attention to the log in your own eye? How can you say to your brother, 'Please brother, let me take the speck out

of your eye,' yet cannot even see the log in your own eye? You hypocrite! First take the log out of your own eye, and then you will be able to see clearly to take the speck out of your brother's eye.

Luke 6:41–42

Jesus saw how easy it is to criticize other people and blame them when things go wrong; it's like seeing bits of dirt in their eyes.

But he surprised everyone by adding that we should pay more attention to our own faults. Just like someone with a big plank sticking out of their eye should take it out before offering to help a friend who's got a speck of dust in theirs!

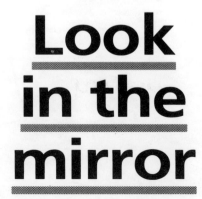

Look in the mirror

Sometimes we can't see the things that are wrong with us. Like planks in our eyes, they stop us seeing clearly, although they're very obvious to other people.

Very often it's the things that we don't like in others that we're most guilty of ourselves. Look back at your list and compare the things that you don't like in other people with your own character.

Lord Jesus, you know how good I am at seeing what's wrong with other people. Please teach me to see what's wrong with myself. Please help me to change. Amen.

Jesus said that we should start with ourselves when we want to put the world right. Write on this log what you think is your biggest fault or bad habit (greedy, lying, selfish, cruel . . .).

Ask a close friend or someone in your family if they agree. Keep asking God to change you.

18

Write down the names of your two favourite stars. What makes them so great?

...B. 9. + ... O. B. ....

....

Read Luke 9:46–48

> *An argument broke out among the disciples as to which of them was the greatest. Jesus knew what they were thinking, so he took a child, stood him by his side, and said to them, 'Whoever welcomes this child in my name, welcomes me; and whoever welcomes me, also welcomes the one who sent me. For he who is least among you all is the greatest.'*

The disciples had got it wrong again! They all wanted to be the greatest. They wanted to feel important and special.

Jesus was brilliant at helping the disciples follow him. He didn't give them a long lecture about being humble. He grabbed their attention by inviting a small child to join them. *'What's Jesus doing?'* they thought. *'Important people like him don't bother to talk to kids.'*

But Jesus was saying, *'Forget your big dreams of being great and important. Care for the people around you who everyone looks down on. That's the way to be great! Doing this is*

one way to show you love me and my Father in heaven.'

Complete this 'Guide to being great' by rearranging the jumbled letters.

Guide to being great in the eyes of the world	Guide to being great in the eyes of God
Put yourself IRSTF. F.I.R.9.T	Put yourself ASLT. .L.A.S.T
GNERIO .I.G.N.O.R.E. people who are unimportant	CWEMELO .W.E.L.C.O.M.E people who are unimportant
Follow EFMA ..F.A.M.E.	Follow EUJSS ..J.E.S.O.S
Build your NOIRPUETTA .R.E.P.U.T.A.T.IO.N	Build up God's ONKGIMD ..K.I.N.G.D.O.M
Make as much YOMEN.m.o.n.e.y as possible	Make as much EACPE. .p.e.a.c.e as possible

Lord Jesus, thank you for teaching me that being great is all about putting others first. Please help me to follow your example, to care for and welcome those who are despised.

Amen.

Who's the greatest?

19

Do I know you?

Jesus' reply started like this:

> 'There was once a man who was going down from Jerusalem to Jericho when robbers attacked him, stripped him, and beat him up, leaving him half dead. It so happened that a priest was going down that road; but when he saw the man, he walked on by, on the other side. In the same way a Levite also came along, went over and looked at the man, and then walked on by, on the other side.'

Luke 10:30–32

'Who is my neighbour?' a lawyer once asked Jesus. He wasn't testing Jesus to see if he knew who lived next door. He wanted Jesus to give him a list (hopefully not too long) of people that he should be nice to.

The priest and the Levite were two of the most respected people around. Good, honest, and faithful to God. So why do you think they left the man dying on the side of the road?

☑ they were scared that the robbers would beat them up as well

☐ they didn't know anything about First Aid

☑ they didn't want to dirty themselves by touching a dead body

☐ they were in a hurry

☐ they thought he was dead

☐ they were unsure who he was—you shouldn't help strangers

You would have thought that these two religious people would have helped.

But religion got in the way of them helping. Touching a wounded or dead body would have made them unclean. They were more concerned with themselves than someone who needed help. Sometimes religion can come between people. What examples can you think of in the world?

N. Ireland and

Bosnia.

There are millions of people in the world today who need help as much as the person in the story. What stops us from giving them help?

☐ I don't know who they are

☑ I'm afraid of what might happen to me

☐ I only want to help certain kinds of people

☐ There's nothing I can do

Lord Jesus, please forgive me for sometimes ignoring other people who are in trouble. Please show me what I can do to help. Amen.

20

Who might be following the priest and Levite on the road? A soldier, a salesman, a kind-hearted traveller? No. Jesus shocked the Jewish lawyer by introducing a despised Samaritan as the hero of the story. (Imagine a new 'RoboCop' film comes out—but this time the RoboCop helps old ladies across the road, and likes ice-cream. What a shock!)

'But a Samaritan who was travelling that way came upon the man, and when he saw him, his heart was filled with pity. He went over to him, poured oil and wine on his wounds and bandaged them; then he put the man on his own animal and took him to an inn, where he took care of him. The next day he took out two silver coins and gave them to the innkeeper. "Take care of him," he told the innkeeper, "and when I come back this way, I will pay you whatever else you spend on him." ' And Jesus concluded, 'In your opinion, which one of these three acted like a neighbour towards the man attacked by the robbers?' The teacher of the Law answered, 'The one who was kind to him.' Jesus replied, 'You go, then, and do the same.'

Luke 10:33–37

The Samaritan did all the things that the priest and Levite did not do. Find four words in this square that describe his actions:

A	C	C	S	G	C	W	Y
B	A	N	D	A	G	E	D
F	R	B	W	V	J	T	E
H	E	S	Z	E	G	F	Q
Z	Q	Y	T	I	P	T	P

1. bandaged
2. gave
3. pity
4. care

He risked his own life to save a stranger. He paid for him to be cared for, and promised to come back to check on him.

The lawyer's question to Jesus was 'Who is my neighbour?' Jesus used the Samaritan in the story to show that your 'neighbour' can be anybody. Not just the people that you know, like, trust, or live next door to! That might be someone you've never met who needs your help. Or people that you do know but never think about—because they're too old, too young, a different race, or from another part of the world.

Lord, God, I'm sorry for being choosy about the people I love. Thank you for the love you have shown me. Please make me strong to love other people in the same way. Amen.

Thought: In answer to the question Jesus turns the idea of a 'neighbour' on its head. Jesus shows a 'neighbour' is someone who gives, not the person who receives.

Jesus told the lawyer to 'go, then, and do the same'. How could your church/youth group be a neighbour to others in the way Jesus describes?

A real neighbour

Think back to the last time you were upset by a close friend or someone in your family:

Why were you hurt? . . . .

. . . .

How did you react?

- ☐ angry
- ☐ wanted to get your own back
- ☐ bitter
- ☐ wanted to sort things out

 Jesus told a story about a father and two sons. Both sons hurt their father deeply, but in different ways:

There was once a man who had two sons. The younger one said to him, 'Father, give me my share of the property now.' So the father divided his property between his two sons. After a few days the younger son sold his part of the property and left home with the money. He went to a country far away, where he wasted his money in reckless living. He spent everything he had. Then a severe famine spread over that country, and he was left without a thing. So he went to work for one of the citizens of that country, who sent him out to his farm to take care of the pigs. He wished he could fill himself with the bean pods the pigs ate, but no one gave him anything to eat. At last he came to his senses and said, 'All my father's hired workers have more than

they can eat, and here I am about to starve! I will get up and go to my father and say, Father, I have sinned against God and against you. I am no longer fit to be called your son; treat me as one of your hired workers.' So he got up and started back to his father.

Luke 15:11–16

The younger son in the story was incredibly rude to his father. He was saying, 'Dad, I wish you were dead. Give me half your life-savings, so I can spend it all on myself, now.'

How would you have felt if you were his father?

I can live

- ☐ glad to be rid of him
- ☑ hurt, and sorry to see him go
- ☐ angry—how could he be so rude
- ☐ worried that you couldn't pay the bills
- ☑ worried what other people would think

The younger son spent the money quickly, and on himself. He ended up alone, hungry and sad. He thought he had ruined his relationship with his father forever.

This is a clear picture of how we treat God. Our attitude is: *'We'll take all the good things that you can give us, but we don't want you! You might as well not exist.'*

22

With each step nearer home, the young man grew more nervous. He had insulted his father, and wasted his savings. Now he dared to come back and ask for a job! Suddenly, he saw someone striding towards him. It was his father, waving his arms in the air. The young man stopped, unsure what to do next. His father ran up, paused, and *smack, hit him hard across the face. 'How dare you show your face here? You wished me dead! Now clear off, and never come back!'*

That was the ending that people listening to Jesus expected. But the father does something quite different:

He was still a long way from home when his father saw him; his heart was filled with pity, and he ran, threw his arms round his son, and kissed him. 'Father', the son said, 'I have sinned against God and against you. I am no longer fit to be called your son.' But the father called his servants. 'Hurry!' he said. 'Bring the best robe and put it on him. Put a ring on his finger and shoes on his feet. Then go and get the prize calf and kill it, and let us celebrate with a feast! For this son of mine was dead, but now he is alive; he was lost, but now he has been found.' And so the feasting began.

Luke 15:20–24

Are you surprised at what the father did? Why?

No, because he would be very happy to see his son again

The father showed that he had completely forgiven his son. He didn't wait for him to reach home and say how sorry he was. He ran down the road with open arms to welcome him back!

Jesus meant this story to show how God is waiting to welcome back anyone who ruins their life. No matter what they've done.

Jesus compares receiving God's forgiveness to being found after you have lost your way. It's more than just a feeling of relief. You were in danger but now you're safe. You have the great joy of being reunited with someone who loves you.

Dear Lord and Father, thank you so much for welcoming me back so enthusiastically when I ask for your forgiveness. Thank you for your patient love for me. Amen.

Welcome home!

23

The elder son in Jesus's story had stayed at home while his younger brother was away:

In the meantime the elder son was out in the field. On his way back, when he came close to the house, he heard the music and dancing. So he called one of the servants and asked him, 'What's going on?' 'Your brother has come back home,' the servant answered, 'and your father has killed the prize calf, because he got him back safe and sound.' The elder brother was so angry that he would not go into the house; so his father came out and begged him to come in. But he answered his father, 'Look, all these years I have worked for you like a slave, and I have never disobeyed your orders. What have you given me? Not even a goat for me to have a feast with my friends! But this son of yours wasted all your property on prostitutes, and when he comes back home, you kill the prize calf for him!' 'My son', the father answered, 'you are always here with me, and everything I have is yours. But we had to celebrate and be happy, because your brother was dead, but now he is alive; he was lost, but now he has been found.'

Luke 15:25–32

In this word square are five words used by or about the elder son. Try to find them

```
E T U X W M
V A N G R Y
A K E L U Z
L P V J C X
S R E D R O
I O R B T H
```

angry ✓
slave ✓
never ✓
orders ✓
my ✓

All the time his brother was away, the elder son had respected his father. He *never* spent money on wild parties. He worked hard and did what he was told.

But he shows that he was as lost as his brother. He was *angry*. All these years he had thought of himself as a *slave* carrying out his father's *orders*, not a son enjoying life at home. He overlooked his father's kindness to him.

Sometimes we think that only 'bad' people need to ask God for forgiveness. People like the younger son who are selfish and reckless. Jesus put the elder son in this story to show that it is possible to look good on the outside, and be full of bitterness and jealousy on the inside.

Everyone needs God's forgiveness. The good news is that, like the father in the story, God is waiting to give it whenever we ask.

Jesus leaves the story unfinished. He doesn't say whether the elder son joins the party. Which of these four endings do you think is the most likely?

- ☐ The elder brother stormed off in a huff
- ☐ The elder brother asked for his father's forgiveness, and went inside to welcome back his brother
- ☑ Father and son went into the party arm-in-arm and enjoyed the celebrations
- ☐ The elder brother joined the party. But only because his father asked him to.

Almighty Father—sometimes I act good on the outside when inside I'm interested only in myself. Please forgive me. Thank you. Amen.

Party pooper

24

Read Luke 18:10–13

Once there were two men who went up to the Temple to pray; one was a Pharisee, the other a tax collector. The Pharisee stood apart by himself and prayed, 'I thank you God, that I am not greedy, dishonest, or an adulterer, like everybody else. I thank you that I am not like that tax collector over there. I fast two days a week, and I give you a tenth of all my income.' But the tax collector stood at a distance and would not even raise his face to heaven, but beat on his breast and said, 'God have pity on me, a sinner!'

The characters in Jesus' story prayed in two different ways. Unscramble the letters to show the difference:

The Pharisee	Tax collector
DROUP PROUN of himself	MELBUH HUMBLE
OBDESAT boasted about himself	KSAS ASKS... for God's mercy
OKOLS LOOKS down on others	LLCAS CALLS himself a sinner

If you had been sitting in the temple, listening to the Pharisee and the tax collector, which one would you have thought was praying the way God wants?

☑ The tax collector, because he was humble in front of God
☐ The Pharisee, because he did lead a good life
☐ Neither of them

Read Luke 18:14

'I tell you,' said Jesus, 'the tax collector, and not the Pharisee, was in the right with God when he went home. For everyone who makes himself great will be humbled, and everyone who humbles himself will be made great.'

Jesus surprised the crowd by saying that the tax collector, not the Pharisee, went home right with God. That is, the traitor, the one who swindled his own people, rather than the good, religious man.

Jesus showed that God accepts the prayers of people who are humble and who know they need forgiveness. It is not good enough to lead a life that has some good points from the outside, but to be full of hot air about how great you are.

Lord Jesus, you know me very well. Please forgive me for the things that I have done wrong. And the good things I haven't done. Please go on making me clean inside. Amen.

Hot air

25

Read Luke 19:38

'God bless the king who comes in the name of the Lord! Peace in heaven and glory to God!'

The crowds shouted and waved madly as Jesus came towards Jerusalem. Here was their great king!

Which word(s) do you think would best describe how Jesus felt?

☐ honoured
☐ proud
☐ angry
☑ sad
☑ happy
☐ grateful
☐ other

Read Luke 19:41–44

He came closer to the city, and when he saw it, he wept over it, saying, 'If you only knew today what is needed for peace! But now you cannot see it! The time will come when your enemies will surround you with barricades, blockade you, and close in on you from every side. They will completely destroy you and the people within your walls; not a single stone will they leave in place, because you did not recognize the time when God came to save you!'

Jesus saw through the loud cheers. The crowd thought that shouting for Jesus as king would be enough to bring peace to the city. Maybe even to get rid of the Roman soldiers they hated so

No peace

much. But they had ignored Jesus' offer of forgiveness, which is the only way to find peace. They ignored the things he did and said which showed that he was God's Son, come to bring peace to the world.

So he cried. He cried, openly without shame. His tears showed his sorrow at the empty praise of the crowds. Not tears for himself, as if he had got it wrong, but tears for the people who shouted so loudly for him and yet had already rejected him and the offer of his love. He cried because he knew that Jerusalem itself, and those living there, would be destroyed as a sign of their rejecting his message.

Jerusalem was destroyed by Roman armies forty years later.

The peace that Jesus gives helps us to get the better of being scared of God, or worrying that he is not interested in us. This doesn't mean that you'll never be sad, angry, or in trouble. It means that whether life is brilliant or difficult, you know that nothing can blot out God's love and forgiveness.

Think of a friend who does not want Jesus' offer of peace. Pray that God will help them to understand it. Pray that they will accept it.

Almighty God, your Son Jesus cried when he saw people shouting that he was their king but ignoring his gift of peace. Please give me the same love for those who don't want to know you.
Amen.

Jesus did a lot of praying. He would often go off to a quiet place to pray (Mark 1:35), or spend the whole night in prayer at important times (Luke 6:12). He astonished his disciples by calling God 'Abba' (which means 'Dear Father, ') as he prayed. He seemed so close to God. He taught them to pray in the same way (Luke 11:2–4).

Just before he was arrested, Jesus went out to pray with his disciples:

Then he went off from them about the distance of a stone's throw and knelt down and prayed. 'Father,' he said, 'If you will, take this cup of suffering away from me. Not my will, however, but your will be done.'

Luke 22:41–42

Jesus faced the physical and spiritual pain of being crucified. Physical, because crucifixion is one of the most painful ways to die ever thought up. Spiritual, because for the first time, Jesus would be cut off from his Father. Jesus went through hell as he took to himself all the evil things that cut people off from God.

In his prayer, Jesus is totally honest. He's not afraid to tell his Father of his fear. But he's concerned only for what his Father wants. That's why he was not afraid to go through with the pain.

Both these things, honesty and willingness to serve God, should be part of all our prayers.

Jesus knelt down when he prayed, even though it was common to stand to pray at that time. This showed that he was serious about saying 'Your will be done '.

Find a quiet place. Kneel down. Offer up to God the things that concern you. Difficult decisions you must make. Things you don't understand. Friends who are ill or suffering. Tell God why they concern you.

For each one, pray, 'Not my will, however, but your will be done '.

Jesus prays

That particular day, the Roman soldiers had three people to put to death. Two local criminals, and a wandering prophet called Jesus of Nazareth. The first two were like all the rest. Hate flashing in their eyes. Fear too. They spat, kicked, and swore loudly. Who could blame them?

Jesus was different. It was funny at first. '*This man thinks he's some sort of king,*' the centurion had told them. So they played a little game. They made a crown of long, sharp thorns and rammed it on top of his head. '*O great king Jesus . . .*' they all laughed. How could this man be a king?

But he was very quiet. He didn't swear, kick, or spit. Even when they flogged him.

Anyway, they didn't have much time to think about it. They had a job to do—it was time to put the three men to death.

Read Luke 23:33–34

When they came to the place called 'The Skull,' they crucified Jesus there, and the two criminals, one on his right and the other on his left. Jesus said, 'Forgive them, Father! They don't know what they are doing.'

Crucifying someone meant nailing their arms and feet to two big planks of wood. Then hauling them up in the air, and leaving them to die of hunger, pain and exhaustion.

Imagine you were one of the soldiers putting Jesus to death. What would you have thought when you heard Jesus say, '*Forgive them, Father!* '?

- ☐ Poor bloke—he's finally gone mad—he's talking nonsense
- ☒ It's much easier to do this job when they put up a fight—you don't feel so bad

I WONDER WHO HE REALLY IS?

☑ I don't need forgiving—I'm just following orders

☒ How can he think about forgiving people at a time like this? Why's he so concerned about us?

Jesus talked to his disciples about forgiveness many times. He taught them to pray, '*Forgive us our sins, for we forgive everyone who does us wrong.*' Now, at the darkest time of his life, he refused to hate the people who killed him. Instead, he forgave them.

Jesus forgives

Almighty God, I find it easy to hold on to the hatred and hurt that I sometimes feel. Please give me the strength to forgive the people who hurt me. Thank you for so often forgiving me. Amen.

Which of these is the odd one out?

- [ ] criminal
- [ ] sentence
- [ ] punishment
- [ ] execution
- [x] king
- [ ] prison

The sign that was nailed to the cross of Jesus read '*This is the King of the Jews*.' It gave the soldiers who put Jesus to death something to laugh about. '*If you're such a great king, save yourself!*' they mocked.

One of the criminals hanging there hurled insults at him: 'Aren't you the Messiah? Save yourself and us!' The other one, however, rebuked him, saying 'Don't you fear God? You received the same sentence he did. Ours, however, is only right, because we are getting what we deserve for what we did; but he has done no wrong.' And he said to Jesus, 'Remember me, Jesus, when you come as King!' Jesus said to him, 'I promise you that today you will be in Paradise with me.'

Luke 23:39–43

The first criminal thought like the soldiers. Even as he died he made fun of Jesus. He knew that Jesus had been welcomed as the Messiah, God's anointed one. But he didn't look like a Messiah or a king now, did he?

The second criminal saw things differently. He knew that he deserved to be put to death. There had been no false justice for him. But Jesus had done nothing wrong—nothing to deserve this terrible death.

He saw the truth in the sign '*The King of the Jews*'. He didn't completely understand who Jesus was. But he sensed that Jesus could help him. He knew, in his last moments, that in fact, only Jesus could help him once he died.

He too was surprised by Jesus. That very day they would be together in heaven. Jesus the king promised this.

The criminal didn't look like a religious man. But like many people who met Jesus, including lawyers, prostitutes, fishermen, beggars, he was amazed by Jesus' love and offer of peace. He discovered that Jesus welcomes all sorts of people into his kingdom, even if they turn to him only at the last moment.

Jesus the King

Lord Jesus, you are the king of life and death. Thank you that because you died, I don't need to be scared about dying. Thank you that one day I will be with you in heaven. Amen.

Read Luke 24:1–3

> Very early on Sunday morning the women went to the tomb, carrying spices they had prepared. They found the stone rolled away from the entrance to the tomb, so they went in; but they did not find the body of the Lord Jesus.

The tomb of Jesus was empty, only three days after he was buried. What had happened? Where had his body gone? There are three possibilities.

The first is that the disciples took the body. To do this, they got past the guards watching the tomb, took the body, and hid it somewhere else. (Not that easy!) Then, several weeks later, they shocked Jerusalem by saying that Jesus was alive. They had seen him! They kept up their story, even when they were beaten and put in prison. Some of them were killed.

This makes no sense. Why would they go through all that hassle and cruel persecution to back up one huge lie?

The second is that some of Jesus' enemies, probably the religious leaders, stole the body. They had no reason to. They already had Jesus exactly where they wanted him: dead, buried and under guard! When the disciples started saying, *'Jesus is alive! We've seen him,'* they could have said, *'Jesus is dead! Here's his body to prove it!'*

But they never did. Instead, they had to make up the story that the guards fell asleep, and that the disciples crept off with the body.

The tomb was definitely empty.

Luke gives the third answer:

> They stood there puzzled about this, when suddenly two men in bright shining clothes stood by them. Full of fear, the women bowed down to the ground, as the men said to them, 'Why are you looking among the dead for one who is alive? He is not here; he has been raised. Remember what he said to you while he was in Galilee: "The Son of Man must be handed over to sinful men, be crucified, and three days later rise to life."'
>
> Luke 24:4–7

Jesus had died. But that was not the end. The tomb was empty because he had risen from the dead. Just like he said he would.

The people Luke wrote his Gospel for believed that when you die your body decayed and your soul was set free. Why did Luke make it difficult for people to believe the Christian faith by saying that the body of Jesus lived on beyond death? The answer: that's what happened!

Lord Jesus, it's so great that you're alive, that you left the tomb empty on the first Easter morning. Thank you that you're not a dead hero but a living king. Amen.

Where is he?

Two of Jesus' disciples were travelling to a village called Emmaus, outside Jerusalem, and talking about his death three days earlier:

As they talked and discussed, Jesus himself drew near and walked along with them; they saw him, but somehow did not recognize him. Jesus said to them, 'What are you talking about to each other, as you walk along?' They stood still, with sad faces. One of them, named Cleopas, asked him, 'Are you the only visitor in Jerusalem who doesn't' know the things that have been happening there these last few days?' 'What things?' he asked. 'The things that happened to Jesus of Nazareth,' they answered. 'This man was a prophet and was considered by God and by all the people to be powerful in everything he said and did. Our chief priests and rulers handed him over to be sentenced to death, and he was crucified. And we had hoped that he would be the one who was going to set Israel free!'

Luke 24:15–21

The two disciples had hoped that Jesus would free their country from Roman occupation. But their hopes had been blown away—Jesus was dead.

Their problem was that they thought Jesus' death was a disaster. They thought that everything had been going well. Then suddenly Jesus had been caught out by the chief priests and killed. They were wrong.

Then Jesus said to them, 'How foolish you are, how slow you are to believe everything the prophets said! Was it not necessary for the Messiah to suffer these things and then to enter his glory?' And Jesus explained to them what was said about himself in all the Scriptures, beginning with the books of Moses and the writings of all the prophets.

Luke 24:25–27

So why did Jesus have to suffer?

Firstly, because the Old Testament prophets had said he would. God showed them that the Messiah ('God's Anointed One') would first suffer and then rule as king. The disciples had only taken in the bit about the great king.

Secondly, it was only by suffering in our place that he could carry out God's rescue plan for the world. Jesus knew that we couldn't get rid of sin by ourselves. Sin cuts us off from God. That's why it's so serious. So, Jesus took to himself all the sins of the world. It was painful and lonely because our sins cut him off from God his Father.

Imagine you steal a car. At first it's great fun burning around, pulling handbrake turns and impressing your friends. But suddenly 'Wham!' The car spins out of control and smashes into a wall. It's a write-off. Weeks later you hear the judge sum up the case. 'You have been reckless. You must pay a fine of £15,000. Case dismissed!' And just as you're wondering how you'll ever pay up, the judge stands. He takes out a cheque book, writes a cheque for £15,000, and hands it to you.
He has paid the price for something you did.

Jesus proved that we are worth far more than the price of a car. His death showed that God was willing to give up everything to pay the price for our freedom. There was no other way.

But that was not all. Jesus was now alive and walking with the disciples on the road. That was the proof that he was not just some great prophet or leader; he was God's Son.

Lord Jesus, Thank you that you died so that I could live forever. Thank you that your death was not an accident or disaster. You are alive! You are my Saviour! Amen.

No other way!

31

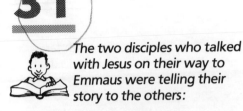

The two disciples who talked with Jesus on their way to Emmaus were telling their story to the others:

Suddenly the Lord himself stood among them and said to them, 'Peace be with you.' They were terrified, thinking that they were seeing a ghost. But he said to them, 'Why are you alarmed? Why are these doubts coming up in your minds? Look at my hands and my feet, and see that it is I myself. Feel me, and you will know, for a ghost doesn't have flesh and bones, as you can see I have.' He said this and showed them his hands and his feet. They still could not believe, they were so full of joy and wonder; so he asked them, 'Have you anything here to eat?' They gave him a piece of cooked fish, which he took and ate in their presence.

Luke 24:36b–43

Jesus had surprised the disciples many times. But this was the most amazing of all! They didn't know whether to be scared or to celebrate. What was going on?

Jesus convinced them that he really had risen from the dead. First, there were the nailmarks in his hands and feet, showing how he had been killed three days before. Then, Jesus let the disciples touch him. He wasn't a ghost, but made of skin and bone just like them. Last of all, he ate a piece of fish in front of them. Ghosts do not eat fish!

Jesus knew that the disciples were shocked and confused. Patiently and firmly he showed that he was alive again, not as a kindly spook, but a real person.

But there is nothing surprising about Jesus rising from the dead. He said all along that he would first be killed and then rise again (read Luke 9:22). It proved that his death was not a failure. For if Jesus had stayed dead, how could anyone say that he's the Saviour—the one who rescues us from death? But because we know that Jesus did rise again, we can be sure that he can save us too.

Jesus had shown God's power as he healed people and set them free from their sin. His rising from the dead was the greatest sign of his power.

That is not the end of the story. It is the beginning. Because we know that God raised Jesus from the dead, we know that he will do the same for us. That same power is available now to start making us more like Jesus.

Read the passage again.

Imagine you are with the disciples. What do you want to say to Jesus?

It's me!

Lord Jesus, by myself I am weak. I want to be more like you. Please fill me with your power. Please set me free from my sin. Amen.

32

What next?

The Following Jesus Series

If you have enjoyed using *Surprised by Jesus* , you might like to look at other titles in the series. All are available singly or in packs of 10 copies.

Following Jesus presents a lively and stimulating introduction to the Christian faith in words and cartoons. Suitable for use as a confirmation course, the 31 steps/ units (with practical suggestions and prayers) cover the basics of Christian teaching and discipleship. An additional leaflet is available which provides leaders with suggestions for four weekly sessions.

Serving Jesus tackles many of the questions and problems facing young people as they try to serve Jesus. A further 27 units are presented, each linked with a character or event from the New Testament and including a short Bible reading and prayer. *Serving Jesus* will be particularly suitable for those who have just been confirmed.

Praying with Jesus presents 28 units which each explore one aspect of 'praying with Jesus', with a Bible reading, comment and short assignment. *Praying with Jesus* will appeal to confirmation and post-confirmation candidates and any person anxious to learn more about prayer.

The Power of Jesus contains 28 units which consider the power of Jesus as seen in the seven signs in John's Gospel.

Picturing Jesus contains 28 units which consider the seven 'I Am' sayings in John's Gospel—the pictures which Jesus used to illustrate and show who he was: 'I am the Good Shepherd', 'I am the Vine', I am the Bread of Life', 'I am the Way, the Truth and the Life', 'I am the Light of the World', 'I am the Resurrection and the Life', 'I am the Gate'.

Stories by Jesus contains 31 units which consider ways Jesus used parables to illustrate his teaching and shows how they still relate to and challenge us 2000 years later.

Another 5 titles are planned in the *Following Jesus* series.

All titles in the series are illustrated throughout by Taffy.

Following Jesus, Serving Jesus, Praying with Jesus, The Power of Jesus, Picturing Jesus and *Stories by Jesus* are available now from all good Christian bookshops, or in case of difficulty from BRF, Peter's Way, Sandy Lane West, Oxford, OX4 5HG.

If you would like to know more about the full range of Bible reading notes and other Bible reading group study materials published by BRF, write and ask for a free catalogue.